I0007769

Python for Generative AI: Practical Techniques,

Applications, and Code Examples

What is Generative AI?

Generative AI refers to a subset of artificial

intelligence (AI) that focuses on creating new data

rather than analyzing existing data or making predictions based on it. In other words, instead of just recognizing patterns in data like traditional AI systems, generative AI can actually generate new content, such as images, text, music, or even entire videos, that mimic or resemble human-created content.

Historical Context and Evolution

The roots of generative AI can be traced back to various fields like computer graphics, computational creativity, and machine learning. Over the years, advancements in deep learning and neural networks have greatly accelerated the development of generative AI techniques, making it possible to create increasingly realistic and sophisticated content.

Key Applications and Use Cases

Generative AI has a wide range of applications across various industries. For example, in art and design, it can be used to create digital artwork, generate new music compositions, or even design virtual landscapes. In healthcare, generative models can assist in medical imaging or drug discovery. In entertainment, they can be used for special effects in movies or for generating game environments. Additionally, generative AI has applications in natural language processing (NLP), where it can generate human-like text or dialogue.

Foundations of Generative Models

To understand generative AI, it's important to have a solid grasp of the foundations of generative models. This includes understanding basic concepts in machine learning and deep learning, such as how neural networks function and how they are trained. Generative models are a class of neural networks specifically designed to generate new data samples that resemble a given dataset. They are trained on large datasets and learn to capture the underlying distribution of the data, allowing them to generate new samples that are similar to the training data.

Basics of Machine Learning and Deep Learning

Machine learning is a field of AI that focuses on algorithms that can learn from and make predictions or decisions based on data. Deep learning is a subset of machine learning that uses neural networks with multiple layers to learn complex patterns in data. Understanding these basics is crucial for understanding how generative models work.

Overview of Neural Networks

Neural networks are computational models inspired by the structure and function of the human brain. They consist of interconnected nodes, or neurons, organized into layers. Each neuron performs a simple computation, and the connections between neurons allow information to flow through the network.

Neural networks are capable of learning complex patterns in data and are the foundation of many generative models.

Introduction to Generative Models

Generative models are a class of neural networks that are trained to generate new data samples that resemble a given dataset. They learn to capture the underlying distribution of the data and generate new samples that are similar to the training data. Generative models have applications in various domains, including image generation, text generation, and music generation.

Types of Generative Models

There are several types of generative models, each with its own strengths and weaknesses. Some of the most common types include Variational Autoencoders (VAEs), Generative Adversarial Networks (GANs), Autoregressive Models, and Flow-based Models. Each of these models has its own unique architecture and training procedure, but they all share the common goal of generating new data samples.

Variational Autoencoders (VAEs)

Variational Autoencoders (VAEs) are a type of generative model that combines elements of both autoencoders and probabilistic graphical models. VAEs learn to encode input data into a lower-dimensional latent space, where they then generate new data samples. VAEs are trained using a variational inference framework, which allows them to learn a probability distribution over the latent space.

Theory and Architecture

The architecture of a VAE consists of an encoder network, which maps input data to a latent space, and a decoder network, which generates new data samples from points in the latent space. The encoder and decoder networks are trained simultaneously using a combination of reconstruction loss and a regularization term that encourages the latent space to follow a specific distribution, typically a Gaussian distribution.

Applications and Examples

VAEs have been used in a wide range of applications, including image generation, image inpainting (filling in missing parts of an image), and data compression. They are particularly well-suited to tasks where capturing uncertainty in the data is important, such as in medical imaging or anomaly detection.

Generative Adversarial Networks (GANs)

Generative Adversarial Networks (GANs) are a type of generative model that consists of two neural networks: a generator and a discriminator. The generator network generates new data samples, while the discriminator network tries to distinguish between real data samples and fake samples generated by the generator. GANs are trained using a min-max game framework, where the generator tries to fool the discriminator, and the discriminator tries to correctly classify real and fake samples.

Theory and Architecture

The architecture of a GAN consists of a generator network, which generates new data samples, and a discriminator network, which tries to distinguish between real and fake samples. During training, the generator and discriminator networks are trained iteratively in a adversarial manner, where the generator tries to generate samples that are indistinguishable from real samples, and the discriminator tries to correctly classify real and fake samples.

Applications and Examples

GANs have been used in a wide range of applications, including image generation, image-to-image translation (changing the style or appearance of an image), and data augmentation. They have been particularly successful in generating photorealistic images and have been used in applications such as generating high-resolution images from low-resolution inputs and creating deepfake videos.

Autoregressive Models

Autoregressive models are a class of generative models that model the conditional distribution of each element in a sequence given previous elements. Autoregressive models are typically used for sequential data such as text or time series data. They generate new samples by iteratively sampling from the conditional distribution of each element given the previous elements.

Theory and Architecture

The architecture of an autoregressive model consists of a neural network that takes as input the previous elements in the sequence and outputs the conditional distribution of the next element. During training, the model learns to approximate the conditional distribution of each element given the previous elements using techniques such as masked convolutions or self-attention mechanisms.

Applications and Examples

Autoregressive models have been used in a variety of applications, including text generation, speech synthesis, and music generation. They are particularly well-suited to tasks where the order of elements in the sequence is important, such as generating coherent sentences or melodies.

Flow-based Models

Flow-based models are a class of generative models that learn to transform a simple probability distribution (e.g., a Gaussian distribution) into a more complex distribution that matches the data distribution. Flow-based models achieve this by applying a series of invertible transformations to the input distribution, such that samples from the input distribution can be transformed into samples from the data distribution and vice versa.

Theory and Architecture

The architecture of a flow-based model consists of a series of invertible transformations, typically parameterized by neural networks. During training, the model learns the parameters of the transformations such that samples from the input distribution are transformed into samples from the data distribution. Flow-based models are trained using maximum likelihood estimation or variational inference techniques.

Applications and Examples

Flow-based models have demonstrated success in various applications, including image generation, density estimation, and anomaly detection. In image generation, flow-based models can generate high-quality images with sharp details and realistic textures. In density estimation, these models can accurately estimate the probability density function of a dataset, which is useful for anomaly detection or outlier detection tasks.

Python for Generative AI

Now that we've explored the theoretical foundations

and various types of generative models, it's essential

to dive into practical implementation using Python. Python is widely used in the field of AI and machine learning due to its simplicity, versatility, and extensive libraries. In the following sections, we will cover setting up your Python environment, essential libraries for generative AI, and building your first generative model.

Setting Up Your Python Environment

Before you can start working on generative AI projects, you need to set up your Python environment. This involves installing Python and managing dependencies using package managers like pip or conda. Additionally, you may want to consider using virtual environments to isolate your project dependencies and avoid conflicts with other projects.

Essential Python Libraries for AI

Python offers a rich ecosystem of libraries and frameworks for AI and machine learning. Some of the essential libraries for generative AI include TensorFlow, PyTorch, Keras, NumPy, Pandas, Matplotlib, and Seaborn. These libraries provide tools for building and training neural networks, manipulating data, visualizing results, and more.

Building Your First Generative Model

With your Python environment set up and essential libraries installed, you're ready to build your first generative model. In the upcoming chapters, we'll walk through the process of data preparation and preprocessing, building a simple generative model using TensorFlow or PyTorch, training the model on a dataset, and generating new data samples.

By the end of this book or guide, you'll have a solid understanding of generative AI concepts, practical experience with building and training generative models in Python, and the knowledge to apply generative AI techniques to real-world problems and projects. Let's embark on this journey into the fascinating world of generative AI!

Setting Up Your Python Environment

Setting up your Python environment is the first step towards diving into generative AI. Here's a straightforward guide to get started:

1. **Install Python**: Visit the official Python website (python.org) to download and install the latest version of Python for your operating system.

   shell

   Copy code

   ```shell
   # Installation on Linux/macOS
   $ sudo apt-get install python3
   ```

```
# Installation on Windows
```

Visit python.org and download the installer.

2. **Package Managers**: Utilize package managers like pip or conda to install Python packages and manage dependencies efficiently.

ruby

Copy code

```
# Installation using pip
$ pip install numpy pandas matplotlib seaborn tensorflow torch keras
```

3. **Virtual Environments**: Consider using virtual environments to isolate your project's dependencies and avoid conflicts.

ruby

Copy code

```
# Installation of virtualenv using pip

$ pip install virtualenv


# Create a new virtual environment

$ virtualenv myenv


# Activate the virtual environment

$ source myenv/bin/activate
```

Essential Python Libraries for AI

Python offers a plethora of libraries for AI and machine learning. Here are some essential ones for generative AI:

1. **TensorFlow**: TensorFlow is an open-source machine learning library developed by Google, widely used for building and training deep learning models.

   python

   Copy code

   import tensorflow as tf

2. **PyTorch**: PyTorch is a deep learning framework developed by Facebook's AI Research lab, known for its flexibility and dynamic computation graph.

python

Copy code

import torch

3. **Keras**: Keras is a high-level neural networks API, written in Python and capable of running on top of TensorFlow, Theano, or CNTK. It's known for its user-friendliness and simplicity.

python

Copy code

```
from keras.models import Sequential
from keras.layers import Dense
```

4. **NumPy and Pandas**: NumPy is a fundamental package for scientific computing with Python,

while Pandas provides data structures and data analysis tools.

python

Copy code

```
import numpy as np
import pandas as pd
```

5. **Matplotlib and Seaborn**: Matplotlib is a plotting library for creating static, interactive, and animated visualizations in Python. Seaborn is built on top of Matplotlib and provides a high-level interface for drawing attractive statistical graphics.

python

Copy code

import matplotlib.pyplot as plt

import seaborn as sns

Scenarios and Examples

1. **Scenario**: You're working on an image generation project using TensorFlow.

python

Copy code

import tensorflow as tf

Your TensorFlow code for image generation goes here

2. **Scenario**: You're building a deep learning model for natural language processing using PyTorch.

python

Copy code

```
import torch


# Your PyTorch code for NLP model goes here
```

3. **Scenario**: You're creating a convolutional neural network (CNN) for image classification using Keras.

python

Copy code

```
from keras.models import Sequential
from keras.layers import Conv2D, MaxPooling2D, Flatten, Dense
```

```
# Your Keras code for CNN goes here
```

4. **Scenario**: You're manipulating and analyzing large datasets using NumPy and Pandas.

```python
Copy code
import numpy as np

import pandas as pd


# Your NumPy and Pandas code for data manipulation goes here
```

5. **Scenario**: You're visualizing the performance of your generative model using Matplotlib and Seaborn.

python

Copy code

```python
import matplotlib.pyplot as plt

import seaborn as sns


# Your Matplotlib and Seaborn code for

visualization goes here
```

With these essential Python libraries and tools, you're well-equipped to embark on your journey into the realm of generative AI. Experiment, explore, and unleash your creativity!

6. **Scenario**: You're training a Generative Adversarial Network (GAN) for image generation using TensorFlow.

python

Copy code

```python
import tensorflow as tf

from tensorflow.keras.layers import Dense, Flatten, Reshape

from tensorflow.keras.models import Sequential


# Your TensorFlow code for GAN training goes here
```

7. **Scenario**: You're implementing a variational autoencoder (VAE) for generating handwritten digits using PyTorch.

python

Copy code

```
import torch

import torchvision

from torch import nn, optim

from torch.utils.data import DataLoader


# Your PyTorch code for VAE implementation
goes here
```

8. **Scenario**: You're preprocessing and augmenting image data for training a deep learning model using NumPy and OpenCV.

python

Copy code

```
import numpy as np

import cv2


# Your NumPy and OpenCV code for image

preprocessing goes here
```

9. **Scenario**: You're analyzing the distribution of generated data using statistical techniques with Pandas and SciPy.

python

```
Copy code

import pandas as pd

from scipy.stats import norm


# Your Pandas and SciPy code for statistical

analysis goes here
```

10.   **Scenario**: You're creating interactive visualizations of model predictions using Plotly and Dash.

```python
Copy code

import plotly.graph_objects as go

import dash

import dash_core_components as dcc
```

```
import dash_html_components as html
```

Your Plotly and Dash code for interactive visualizations goes here

These scenarios showcase the versatility and power of Python in the field of generative AI. With the combination of these libraries and tools, you can implement a wide range of generative models, preprocess data efficiently, analyze results, and visualize insights effectively. Experimenting with these libraries will help you gain practical experience and expertise in generative AI.

Data Preparation and Preprocessing

Before building your first generative model, it's crucial to prepare and preprocess your data. This typically involves loading your dataset, performing any necessary transformations or augmentations, and splitting it into training and validation sets. Let's go through an example of preprocessing image data using the popular MNIST dataset:

```python
python

Copy code

import numpy as np

from keras.datasets import mnist

from sklearn.model_selection import train_test_split


# Load the MNIST dataset

(X_train, _), (_, _) = mnist.load_data()


# Normalize pixel values to the range [0, 1]

X_train = X_train.astype('float32') / 255.0


# Reshape the data to fit the input shape of the model

X_train = np.reshape(X_train, (-1, 28, 28, 1))
```

```
# Split the data into training and validation sets

X_train, X_val = train_test_split(X_train, test_size=0.2,

random_state=42)


print("Data preprocessing complete.")
```

This code snippet loads the MNIST dataset, normalizes the pixel values, reshapes the data, and splits it into training and validation sets.

Building a Simple VAE (Variational Autoencoder) in Python

Now, let's build a simple Variational Autoencoder (VAE) using TensorFlow and Keras. VAEs are a type of generative model that learns to encode input data into a lower-dimensional latent space and then

decode it back into the original data space. Here's
how you can implement a VAE:

python

Copy code

```python
import tensorflow as tf

from tensorflow.keras import layers, Model


# Define the VAE architecture
latent_dim = 2


# Encoder
encoder_inputs = tf.keras.Input(shape=(28, 28, 1))

x = layers.Flatten()(encoder_inputs)

x = layers.Dense(256, activation='relu')(x)
```

```python
z_mean = layers.Dense(latent_dim, name='z_mean')(x)
z_log_var             =             layers.Dense(latent_dim,
name='z_log_var')(x)


# Reparameterization trick
def sampling(args):
    z_mean, z_log_var = args
    epsilon                                                =
tf.keras.backend.random_normal(shape=(tf.shape(z_
mean)[0], latent_dim))
    return z_mean + tf.exp(0.5 * z_log_var) * epsilon


z   =   layers.Lambda(sampling,   name='z')([z_mean,
z_log_var])
```

```python
# Decoder
decoder_inputs = layers.Input(shape=(latent_dim,))
x = layers.Dense(256, activation='relu')(decoder_inputs)
x = layers.Dense(28 * 28, activation='sigmoid')(x)
decoder_outputs = layers.Reshape((28, 28, 1))(x)


# Define the VAE model
encoder = Model(encoder_inputs, [z_mean, z_log_var, z], name='encoder')
decoder = Model(decoder_inputs, decoder_outputs, name='decoder')


# VAE model
outputs = decoder(encoder(encoder_inputs)[2])
```

```
vae = Model(encoder_inputs, outputs, name='vae')
```

This code defines the architecture of a VAE using TensorFlow and Keras. It consists of an encoder network, a decoder network, and the reparameterization trick for sampling from the latent space.

Building a Simple GAN (Generative Adversarial Network) in Python

Next, let's build a simple Generative Adversarial Network (GAN) using TensorFlow and Keras. GANs are a type of generative model that consists of two neural networks: a generator and a discriminator, which are trained simultaneously in a game-like fashion. Here's how you can implement a GAN:

```python
Copy code
import tensorflow as tf
from tensorflow.keras import layers, Model


# Generator
latent_dim = 100
generator_input = tf.keras.Input(shape=(latent_dim,))
x = layers.Dense(128 * 7 * 7, activation='relu')(generator_input)
x = layers.Reshape((7, 7, 128))(x)
x = layers.Conv2DTranspose(128, 4, strides=2, padding='same', activation='relu')(x)
x = layers.Conv2DTranspose(64, 4, strides=2, padding='same', activation='relu')(x)
```

```python
generator_output = layers.Conv2D(1, 7,
padding='same', activation='sigmoid')(x)


# Define the generator model
generator = Model(generator_input,
generator_output, name='generator')


# Discriminator
discriminator_input = layers.Input(shape=(28, 28, 1))
x = layers.Conv2D(64, 3, strides=2, padding='same',
activation='relu')(discriminator_input)
x = layers.Conv2D(128, 3, strides=2, padding='same',
activation='relu')(x)
x = layers.Flatten()(x)
x = layers.Dense(1, activation='sigmoid')(x)
```

```python
# Define the discriminator model
discriminator = Model(discriminator_input, x,
name='discriminator')


# GAN model
gan_output =
discriminator(generator(generator_input))
gan = Model(generator_input, gan_output,
name='gan')
```

This code defines the architecture of a GAN using TensorFlow and Keras. It consists of a generator network, a discriminator network, and the GAN model that combines them.

Advanced Techniques and Architectures

Conditional Generative Models

Conditional generative models are capable of generating data samples conditioned on additional input information. For example, given a text description, a conditional image generator can produce an image that corresponds to the description. Let's explore how to implement a conditional image generator using TensorFlow and Keras:

python

Copy code

```
import tensorflow as tf
from tensorflow.keras.layers import Input, Dense, Reshape, Embedding, Concatenate
```

```python
from tensorflow.keras.models import Model


# Define the input placeholders

text_input = Input(shape=(max_text_length,))

label_input = Input(shape=(num_classes,))


# Embed the text input

embedding_layer      =       Embedding(vocab_size,

embedding_dim)(text_input)

embedded_text = Flatten()(embedding_layer)


# Concatenate the embedded text and label input

concatenated_input = Concatenate()([embedded_text,

label_input])
```

```
# Define the generator architecture

# ...


# Define the conditional generator model

conditional_generator  =  Model(inputs=[text_input,

label_input], outputs=generated_image)
```

In this scenario, we're building a conditional image generator that takes text descriptions and labels as input to generate corresponding images. The model architecture would follow a similar structure to a standard generator, but with additional input layers for the text and labels.

StyleGAN and Advanced GAN Variants

StyleGAN is an advanced variant of Generative Adversarial Networks (GANs) known for its ability to generate high-resolution, photorealistic images with fine-grained control over specific attributes like facial expressions, hair styles, and backgrounds. Let's see how to implement StyleGAN using TensorFlow and Keras:

python

Copy code

```
# Implementing StyleGAN with TensorFlow and Keras
# ...


# Code snippet pending...
```

This snippet would involve a more complex architecture than a standard GAN, incorporating techniques such as progressive growing, style mixing, and adaptive instance normalization (AdaIN) to achieve superior image quality and diversity.

Enhancements and Improvements in VAEs

Variational Autoencoders (VAEs) have seen various enhancements and improvements over the years, such as beta-VAEs, disentangled VAEs, and hierarchical VAEs, aimed at improving the quality, diversity, and controllability of generated samples. Let's explore how to implement a beta-VAE for disentangled representation learning using PyTorch:

python

```
Copy code

import torch

import torch.nn as nn

import torch.optim as optim

from torch.utils.data import DataLoader

# Import other necessary modules


# Define the beta-VAE architecture

class BetaVAE(nn.Module):

    def __init__(self, latent_dim):

        super(BetaVAE, self).__init__()

        # Define encoder, decoder, and other necessary
layers


    def forward(self, x):
```

```python
# Define forward pass


# Instantiate the beta-VAE model

vae = BetaVAE(latent_dim)


# Define loss function and optimizer

# Train the beta-VAE model

# Code snippet pending...
```

This code would implement a beta-VAE model in PyTorch, capable of learning disentangled representations of input data, which can be useful for tasks like image manipulation and generation.

Training and Optimization

Data Augmentation Techniques

Data augmentation is a crucial technique in training generative models, especially when dealing with limited or unbalanced datasets. Augmentation techniques like rotation, translation, scaling, and flipping can help increase the diversity and robustness of the training data. Let's implement data augmentation using the TensorFlow Data API:

python

Copy code

```
import tensorflow as tf


# Define data augmentation pipeline
```

```python
data_augmentation = tf.keras.Sequential([

tf.keras.layers.experimental.preprocessing.RandomRo
tation(0.2),

tf.keras.layers.experimental.preprocessing.RandomZo
om(0.2),

tf.keras.layers.experimental.preprocessing.RandomTr
anslation(0.1, 0.1),
    # Add more augmentation layers as needed
])


# Apply data augmentation to the dataset
```

```
augmented_dataset = dataset.map(lambda x, y:
(data_augmentation(x), y))
```

This code snippet demonstrates how to define and apply common data augmentation techniques to an image dataset using TensorFlow's preprocessing layers.

Hyperparameter Tuning

Hyperparameter tuning is essential for optimizing the performance of generative models. Techniques like grid search, random search, and Bayesian optimization can help find the best set of hyperparameters for a given model and dataset. Let's use the scikit-learn library to perform hyperparameter tuning for a convolutional neural network (CNN):

```python
Copy code
from sklearn.model_selection import GridSearchCV
from keras.wrappers.scikit_learn import KerasClassifier


# Define the CNN model architecture
def create_model(activation='relu', optimizer='adam'):
    model = Sequential([
        Conv2D(32, kernel_size=(3, 3), activation=activation, input_shape=input_shape),
        MaxPooling2D(pool_size=(2, 2)),
        Flatten(),
        Dense(128, activation=activation),
        Dense(num_classes, activation='softmax')
```

```python
    ])

    model.compile(loss='categorical_crossentropy',
optimizer=optimizer, metrics=['accuracy'])

    return model


# Define hyperparameters to tune
param_grid = {
    'activation': ['relu', 'tanh'],

    'optimizer': ['adam', 'rmsprop']

}


# Create a KerasClassifier
model    =    KerasClassifier(build_fn=create_model,
epochs=10, batch_size=32, verbose=0)
```

```
# Perform grid search

grid            =            GridSearchCV(estimator=model,

param_grid=param_grid, n_jobs=-1)

grid_result = grid.fit(X_train, y_train)
```

In this example, we use GridSearchCV from scikit-learn to perform a grid search over different combinations of activation functions and optimizers for a CNN model.

Debugging and Improving Model Performance

Debugging and improving model performance often involve techniques like gradient checking, visualization of model internals (e.g., activation maps, gradients), and analyzing misclassified samples. Let's visualize activation maps in a CNN using TensorFlow and Keras:

python

Copy code

```python
import matplotlib.pyplot as plt


# Choose a sample image from the dataset

sample_image = X_train[0]


# Define a model that outputs intermediate layer activations

activation_model = Model(inputs=model.input,
outputs=model.layers[1].output)


# Get the intermediate layer activations for the
sample image
```

```python
activations =
activation_model.predict(sample_image.reshape(1,
28, 28, 1))


# Plot the activation maps
plt.figure(figsize=(10, 10))
for i in range(32):
    plt.subplot(4, 8, i + 1)
    plt.imshow(activations[0, :, :, i], cmap='viridis')
plt.show()
```

This code snippet demonstrates how to visualize activation maps for the first convolutional layer of a CNN model using TensorFlow and Matplotlib.

Evaluation and Metrics for Generative Models

Qualitative Evaluation Methods

Qualitative evaluation methods involve visually inspecting generated samples to assess their quality, diversity, and realism. This can include inspecting individual samples, comparing them to ground truth data, and assessing overall coherence. Let's visualize generated images from a GAN using TensorFlow and Matplotlib:

python

Copy code

```
import matplotlib.pyplot as plt
```

```python
# Generate a batch of images using the trained GAN
model
generated_images = gan.predict(noise_input)


# Plot the generated images
plt.figure(figsize=(10, 10))
for i in range(25):
    plt.subplot(5, 5, i + 1)
    plt.imshow(generated_images[i, :, :, 0], cmap='gray')
    plt.axis('off')
plt.show()
```

In this example, we use a trained GAN model to generate a batch of images from random noise input and visualize them using Matplotlib.

Quantitative Metrics

Quantitative metrics provide numerical measures of the quality, diversity, and other characteristics of generated samples. Common metrics for evaluating generative models include Inception Score (IS), Frechet Inception Distance (FID), and Perceptual Path Length (PPL). Let's compute the Inception Score (IS) for generated images using TensorFlow and Keras:

python

Copy code

```python
import numpy as np


# Generate a batch of images using the trained GAN
model
```

```python
generated_images = gan.predict(noise_input)


# Compute the Inception Score (IS)

def inception_score(images):

    # Compute IS using TensorFlow or other methods

    # Code snippet pending...

    return is_score


is_score = inception_score(generated_images)

print("Inception Score:", is_score)
```

This code snippet demonstrates how to compute the Inception Score (IS) for generated images using TensorFlow or other methods.

Applications of Generative AI

Image Generation and Editing

Generative AI has numerous applications in image generation and editing, including generating photorealistic images, image-to-image translation, and image inpainting. For example, let's use a trained

StyleGAN model to generate high-quality images of human faces:

Text Generation and Natural Language Processing

Generative AI can also be used for text generation tasks such as language modeling, text summarization, and dialogue generation. Let's generate text using a pre-trained language model in the GPT-3 family:

Generating Contextually Accurate Content with Advanced LLM Fine-Tuning

Fine-tuning large language models (LLMs) is a critical step in adapting generative AI to specialized domains. While pre-trained models like GPT-4 have extensive capabilities, they often require domain-specific fine-tuning to achieve optimal performance in specialized applications such as legal documentation, medical diagnoses, or technical content generation. This chapter dives into advanced strategies for fine-tuning, utilizing Python frameworks like PyTorch and Hugging Face Transformers. The focus is on methods that not only improve performance but also minimize computational costs.

Dataset Preparation for Fine-Tuning

The first step in fine-tuning is acquiring and preparing the dataset. The quality of the dataset directly influences the model's performance. A well-prepared dataset ensures accurate and contextually relevant outputs. Python libraries such as pandas, NLTK, and spaCy are instrumental in cleaning, tokenizing, and annotating text data.

Code Example: Cleaning and Tokenizing Data

python

Copy code

```
import pandas as pd

from nltk.tokenize import word_tokenize

from sklearn.model_selection import train_test_split


# Load dataset

data = pd.read_csv('domain_data.csv')


# Clean text
```

```
data['clean_text'] =

data['text'].str.lower().str.replace('[^\w\s]', '')


# Tokenize

data['tokens'] =

data['clean_text'].apply(word_tokenize)


# Split into training and validation sets

train_data, val_data = train_test_split(data,

test_size=0.2, random_state=42)
```

Transfer Learning for Domain Adaptation

Fine-tuning often leverages pre-trained models as a

base, reducing training time while enhancing

performance. Using Hugging Face's transformers

library, the Trainer API simplifies this process. By adjusting hyperparameters and freezing specific layers, you can balance computational efficiency and performance.

Code Example: Fine-Tuning with Hugging Face

python

Copy code

```
from transformers import AutoTokenizer,
AutoModelForCausalLM, Trainer, TrainingArguments


# Load tokenizer and model
tokenizer = AutoTokenizer.from_pretrained("gpt-4")
model =
AutoModelForCausalLM.from_pretrained("gpt-4")
```

```python
# Tokenize data

def tokenize_function(examples):

    return tokenizer(examples['text'], truncation=True,

padding=True, max_length=512)


tokenized_train = train_data.map(tokenize_function,

batched=True)

tokenized_val = val_data.map(tokenize_function,

batched=True)


# Define training arguments

training_args = TrainingArguments(

    output_dir="./results",

    evaluation_strategy="epoch",
```

```python
    learning_rate=2e-5,

    per_device_train_batch_size=4,

    num_train_epochs=3,

    weight_decay=0.01,

    save_total_limit=2,

)


# Initialize Trainer

trainer = Trainer(

    model=model,

    args=training_args,

    train_dataset=tokenized_train,

    eval_dataset=tokenized_val,

)
```

```
# Fine-tune the model

trainer.train()
```

Ensuring Model Robustness with Adversarial Examples

Generative models must withstand adversarial input to ensure reliability. Techniques such as adversarial training improve model robustness. By injecting perturbations during training, you can enhance the model's ability to handle noisy or misleading inputs.

Code Example: Adversarial Training

python

Copy code

```python
from textattack.augmentation import

EmbeddingAugmenter

# Adversarial data augmentation

augmenter = EmbeddingAugmenter()

# Generate adversarial examples

data['adversarial_text'] =

data['clean_text'].apply(lambda x:

augmenter.augment(x))

# Add adversarial examples to the dataset

augmented_data = pd.concat([data['clean_text'],

data['adversarial_text']])
```

Multi-Modal Generative AI: Text, Images, and Beyond

Generative AI has evolved beyond text-based applications. Multi-modal systems combine text, images, and other data types to create richer user experiences. For instance, models like CLIP (Contrastive Language–Image Pre-training) and DALL·E bridge the gap between text and image understanding. Python libraries like OpenAI's API and torchvision make multi-modal generation accessible.

Integrating Text and Image Models

Multi-modal applications often involve integrating language and vision models. For example, creating a captioning system that generates descriptive text for images requires combining LLMs with computer vision models.

Code Example: Image Captioning with Vision and LLMs

python

Copy code

```
from transformers import
VisionEncoderDecoderModel, ViTFeatureExtractor,
AutoTokenizer
from PIL import Image


# Load model and feature extractor
```

```python
model =
VisionEncoderDecoderModel.from_pretrained("nlpco
nnect/vit-gpt2-image-captioning")
feature_extractor =
ViTFeatureExtractor.from_pretrained("google/vit-
base-patch16-224")
tokenizer = AutoTokenizer.from_pretrained("gpt2")


# Load and process image
image = Image.open("sample_image.jpg")
pixel_values = feature_extractor(images=image,
return_tensors="pt").pixel_values


# Generate caption
```

```
output_ids = model.generate(pixel_values,

max_length=16, num_beams=4)

caption = tokenizer.decode(output_ids[0],

skip_special_tokens=True)

print(caption)
```

Cross-Modal Embeddings for Enhanced Understanding

Cross-modal embeddings enable models to align data from different modalities. CLIP is a prime example of this approach. By training on paired text and image data, it learns a shared representation space, enabling applications like image search based on textual descriptions.

Code Example: Using CLIP for Text-to-Image Matching

python

Copy code

```
import torch

from transformers import CLIPProcessor, CLIPModel


# Load CLIP model and processor
model = CLIPModel.from_pretrained("openai/clip-vit-base-patch32")
processor = CLIPProcessor.from_pretrained("openai/clip-vit-base-patch32")
```

```python
# Inputs

image = Image.open("sample_image.jpg")

text = ["a dog", "a cat"]


# Preprocess inputs

inputs = processor(text=text, images=image,

return_tensors="pt", padding=True)


# Generate embeddings

outputs = model(**inputs)

logits_per_image = outputs.logits_per_image

probs = logits_per_image.softmax(dim=1)


print("Probabilities:", probs)
```

Challenges in Multi-Modal Generative AI

Multi-modal systems face challenges, such as aligning representations across modalities, handling large datasets, and optimizing training. Techniques like cross-modal attention and transfer learning address these issues, enabling better integration of text and image data.

Efficient Large-Scale Training with Distributed Systems

Training LLMs and multi-modal models often requires significant computational resources. Distributed training using frameworks like PyTorch's

DistributedDataParallel and TensorFlow's tf.distribute.Strategy allows scaling across multiple GPUs or nodes.

Setting Up Distributed Training

To efficiently utilize hardware, distributed training divides workloads across multiple devices. This ensures faster training and scalability for large models.

Code Example: Distributed Training with PyTorch

python

Copy code

```
import torch
from torch.nn.parallel import DistributedDataParallel as DDP
```

```python
# Initialize process group

torch.distributed.init_process_group("nccl")


# Model setup

model = YourModel().to(device)

ddp_model = DDP(model)


# Optimizer

optimizer =

torch.optim.Adam(ddp_model.parameters(), lr=1e-4)


# Training loop

for epoch in range(num_epochs):

    for batch in dataloader:
```

```
inputs, labels = batch

optimizer.zero_grad()

outputs = ddp_model(inputs)

loss = criterion(outputs, labels)

loss.backward()

optimizer.step()
```

Optimizing Resource Utilization

Techniques like gradient checkpointing and mixed-precision training reduce memory usage and speed up computation. NVIDIA's apex library is a popular choice for implementing these optimizations.

Code Example: Mixed-Precision Training

python

Copy code

```python
from apex import amp


# Initialize model and optimizer
model = YourModel().to(device)
optimizer = torch.optim.Adam(model.parameters(),
lr=1e-4)


# Enable mixed-precision training
model, optimizer = amp.initialize(model, optimizer,
opt_level="O1")


# Training loop
for epoch in range(num_epochs):
    for batch in dataloader:
```

```python
inputs, labels = batch

optimizer.zero_grad()

with amp.autocast():

    outputs = model(inputs)

    loss = criterion(outputs, labels)

amp.scale_loss(loss, optimizer).backward()

optimizer.step()
```

Real-Time Generative AI Applications with Low-Latency Inference

Generative AI models often face challenges when deployed in real-time applications due to their size and computational demands. This chapter explores advanced techniques for optimizing inference latency while maintaining high-quality output. Tools like TensorRT, ONNX Runtime, and model quantization are integral to achieving these goals.

Optimizing Model Inference with Quantization

Quantization reduces model size by representing weights and activations with lower precision, such as

8-bit integers instead of 32-bit floats. This optimization reduces memory and computational requirements, making it ideal for real-time applications.

Code Example: Post-Training Quantization with PyTorch

python

Copy code

```python
import torch
from torch.quantization import quantize_dynamic, get_default_qconfig


# Load pre-trained model
model = torch.load("fine_tuned_model.pth")
```

```python
# Apply dynamic quantization

quantized_model = quantize_dynamic(

    model,  # Model to quantize

    {torch.nn.Linear},  # Layers to quantize

    dtype=torch.qint8  # Data type for quantization

)



# Save the quantized model

torch.save(quantized_model, "quantized_model.pth")
```

Using TensorRT for High-Performance Inference

NVIDIA TensorRT optimizes models for GPU-based

inference, providing significant speedups. It supports

model conversion from frameworks like TensorFlow and PyTorch.

Code Example: Exporting and Running a Model with TensorRT

python

Copy code

```python
import tensorrt as trt

import pycuda.driver as cuda

import pycuda.autoinit


# Load ONNX model

onnx_file_path = "model.onnx"

engine_file_path = "model.trt"
```

```python
# Build TensorRT engine

logger = trt.Logger(trt.Logger.WARNING)

builder = trt.Builder(logger)

network = builder.create_network(trt.NetworkDefinitionCreatio

nFlag.EXPLICIT_BATCH)

parser = trt.OnnxParser(network, logger)


with open(onnx_file_path, "rb") as f:

    parser.parse(f.read())


# Configure and build the engine

config = builder.create_builder_config()

config.max_workspace_size = 1 << 30  # 1GB

engine = builder.build_engine(network, config)
```

```python
# Save the engine

with open(engine_file_path, "wb") as f:

    f.write(engine.serialize())
```

Techniques for Batch and Stream Processing

In real-time systems, combining batch and stream processing is critical for handling fluctuating workloads. Libraries like Ray Serve and TensorFlow Serving allow scaling while maintaining low latency.

Generative AI in Creative Applications: Music, Art, and Storytelling

Generative AI is revolutionizing creative fields, enabling the creation of music, visual art, and narratives. Models like MuseNet, Jukebox, and Stable Diffusion provide powerful capabilities for generating novel content. This chapter explores how to use Python libraries for creative AI applications.

Music Generation with OpenAI's Jukebox

Jukebox is a neural network capable of generating high-fidelity music, complete with lyrics and instrumentation. It uses a hierarchical VQ-VAE architecture for modeling audio data.

Code Example: Generating Music with Jukebox

python

Copy code

```
from jukebox.make_models import make_vqvae, make_prior, make_decoder
from jukebox.hparams import setup_hparams
```

```python
from jukebox.utils.dist_utils import

setup_dist_from_mpi


# Setup environment

setup_dist_from_mpi()

hparams = setup_hparams('small_vqvae')


# Load models

vqvae = make_vqvae(hparams)

prior = make_prior(hparams)

decoder = make_decoder(hparams)


# Generate music

music_sample = prior.sample(conditioning_tokens)
```

Image Generation with Stable Diffusion

Stable Diffusion creates detailed images from textual prompts using a diffusion-based generative process. It supports tasks such as inpainting and style transfer.

Code Example: Generating Images with Diffusers

python

Copy code

```
from diffusers import StableDiffusionPipeline


# Load pre-trained model
pipeline = StableDiffusionPipeline.from_pretrained("CompVis/stable-diffusion-v1-4")
pipeline = pipeline.to("cuda")
```

```
# Generate an image

prompt = "a surreal landscape with floating islands"

image = pipeline(prompt,

num_inference_steps=50).images[0]

# Save the image

image.save("generated_image.png")
```

Storytelling with Narrative-Optimized LLMs

Storytelling LLMs, fine-tuned for narrative coherence and character development, are transforming the way stories are created. Techniques like prompt engineering and chaining enable the creation of multi-chapter narratives.

Code Example: Prompt Engineering for Story Continuation

```python
Copy code
from transformers import pipeline

# Load text generation pipeline
generator = pipeline("text-generation", model="gpt-4")

# Generate story continuation
prompt = "Once upon a time in a distant galaxy, a lone traveler discovered a"
```

```
story = generator(prompt, max_length=200,

num_return_sequences=1)

print(story[0]["generated_text"])
```

Personalized Generative AI: Building User-Specific Models

Generative AI systems tailored to individual users enhance relevance and engagement. Personalization involves incorporating user preferences, behavioral data, and feedback into the model's training and inference processes.

Using Federated Learning for Personalized Models

Federated learning enables personalization by training models on user data locally, preserving privacy. Frameworks like PySyft simplify implementing federated learning workflows.

Code Example: Federated Training with PySyft

python

Copy code

```python
import syft as sy
import torch
from torch import nn, optim


# Create virtual workers
hook = sy.TorchHook(torch)
alice = sy.VirtualWorker(hook, id="alice")
```

```python
bob = sy.VirtualWorker(hook, id="bob")


# Define model

model = nn.Linear(2, 1)


# Distribute model

model = model.send(alice)


# Train locally on Alice's data

data = torch.tensor([[1.0, 2.0], [3.0, 4.0]]).send(alice)

target = torch.tensor([[1.0], [0.0]]).send(alice)

optimizer = optim.SGD(params=model.parameters(),

lr=0.1)

loss_fn = nn.MSELoss()
```

```python
for _ in range(10):

    optimizer.zero_grad()

    output = model(data)

    loss = loss_fn(output, target)

    loss.backward()

    optimizer.step()


# Get updated model

model = model.get()
```

Reinforcement Learning for Adaptive Personalization

Reinforcement learning allows models to adapt dynamically to user behavior. The agent learns by interacting with the user and maximizing long-term engagement.

Code Example: Q-Learning for Personalization

python

Copy code

```python
import numpy as np


# Initialize Q-table

actions = ["recommend_article", "send_notification"]

states = ["user_active", "user_inactive"]

q_table = np.zeros((len(states), len(actions)))


# Parameters

alpha = 0.1  # Learning rate

gamma = 0.9  # Discount factor


# Simulate a reward system

for episode in range(1000):
```

```python
    state = np.random.choice(len(states))  # Current
state

    action = np.random.choice(len(actions))  # Choose
action

    reward = np.random.random()  # Simulated reward

    next_state = np.random.choice(len(states))  # Next
state


    # Update Q-value
    q_table[state, action] = (1 - alpha) * q_table[state,
action] + alpha * (
        reward + gamma * max(q_table[next_state])
    )


print("Trained Q-Table:", q_table)
```

Handling Privacy and Security in Personalization

Balancing personalization with privacy is crucial. Techniques like differential privacy and secure multi-party computation (SMPC) ensure data protection while enabling personalized experiences.

Generative AI for Scientific Discovery and Research

Generative AI is revolutionizing scientific research by automating data analysis, simulating experiments, and generating hypotheses. Advanced models are being used to accelerate breakthroughs in fields like drug discovery, material science, and astrophysics. This chapter delves into practical implementations, tools, and techniques for leveraging generative AI in scientific research.

Accelerating Drug Discovery with Generative Models

Drug discovery involves identifying molecules that interact effectively with biological targets. Generative models like variational autoencoders (VAEs) and reinforcement learning agents are employed to propose novel molecular structures with desired properties.

Code Example: Molecular Generation with RDKit and PyTorch

python

```python
Copy code

from rdkit import Chem

from rdkit.Chem import Draw

import torch

import torch.nn as nn


# Simple VAE for molecule generation

class MoleculeVAE(nn.Module):

    def __init__(self, input_dim, latent_dim):

        super(MoleculeVAE, self).__init__()

        self.encoder = nn.Sequential(

            nn.Linear(input_dim, 128),

            nn.ReLU(),

            nn.Linear(128, latent_dim)

        )
```

```python
        self.decoder = nn.Sequential(

            nn.Linear(latent_dim, 128),

            nn.ReLU(),

            nn.Linear(128, input_dim),

            nn.Sigmoid()

        )


    def forward(self, x):

        z = self.encoder(x)

        x_recon = self.decoder(z)

        return x_recon, z



# Generate and visualize a molecule

smiles = "CCO"  # Ethanol SMILES string

molecule = Chem.MolFromSmiles(smiles)
```

```
Draw.MolToFile(molecule, "molecule.png")
```

The above example demonstrates using generative models to create molecular representations and visualize them. Researchers often couple these methods with simulations to validate their properties.

Generative AI in Material Science

In material science, discovering new compounds with specific properties is computationally expensive. Generative models such as GANs (Generative Adversarial Networks) help design materials by generating crystal structures or optimizing properties like conductivity or tensile strength.

Code Example: Crystal Structure Generation with PyMatGen

python

Copy code

```python
from pymatgen.core import Structure

from pymatgen.symmetry.analyzer import SpacegroupAnalyzer

import random


# Generate a random crystal structure
structure = Structure.from_spacegroup(
    sg=random.randint(1, 230),
    lattice=[3.5, 3.5, 3.5, 90, 90, 90],
    species=["Si"],
```

```
    coords=[[0, 0, 0]]
)
```

```
# Analyze symmetry

analyzer = SpacegroupAnalyzer(structure)

print("Space Group:",

analyzer.get_space_group_symbol())
```

```
# Export structure to CIF file

structure.to(filename="crystal_structure.cif")
```

This script demonstrates generating random crystal structures and saving them in standard formats for further analysis.

AI-Assisted Hypothesis Generation

Generative AI is being used to propose hypotheses by analyzing vast amounts of research data, enabling scientists to focus on validation. Models fine-tuned on domain-specific literature, like those trained on PubMed data, suggest novel ideas by extracting patterns and identifying research gaps.

Code Example: Using GPT for Hypothesis Generation in Research Papers

python

Copy code

```
from transformers import pipeline


# Load GPT model
```

```python
generator = pipeline("text-generation", model="gpt-3.5-turbo")


# Generate hypotheses based on input data
prompt = (
    "Analyze the following research abstract and
propose a hypothesis: "
    "Abstract: Studies show that higher protein intake
leads to faster muscle recovery."
)
hypotheses = generator(prompt, max_length=150,
num_return_sequences=3)


for idx, hypothesis in enumerate(hypotheses):
```

```
    print(f"Hypothesis {idx+1}:",

hypothesis["generated_text"])
```

This example leverages a language model to assist researchers in formulating hypotheses, streamlining the ideation process.

Generative Models for Simulating Scientific Experiments

Simulating experiments using generative AI reduces the need for physical trials, saving time and resources. AI models can predict outcomes based on controlled parameters, assisting in areas like climate modeling and particle physics.

Code Example: Climate Data Simulation with GANs

python

Copy code

```python
import tensorflow as tf

from tensorflow.keras import layers


# Define a simple GAN

def build_generator():

    model = tf.keras.Sequential([

        layers.Dense(128, activation="relu",

input_dim=100),

        layers.Dense(256, activation="relu"),

        layers.Dense(784, activation="sigmoid"),

    ])
```

```python
    return model


def build_discriminator():
    model = tf.keras.Sequential([
        layers.Dense(256, activation="relu",
input_dim=784),
        layers.Dense(128, activation="relu"),
        layers.Dense(1, activation="sigmoid"),
    ])
    return model


# Train the GAN for climate data simulation
generator = build_generator()
discriminator = build_discriminator()
```

```
# Training loop setup (omitted here for brevity)
```

GANs like this can be extended to simulate more complex datasets, such as historical climate patterns or particle interactions.

Ethical Considerations in Scientific AI Applications

While generative AI opens new doors, it raises concerns about reproducibility and misuse in scientific research. Ensuring transparency in model development and adhering to ethical guidelines is critical for maintaining integrity in discoveries.

By integrating generative AI, scientific disciplines gain powerful tools to accelerate research, offering solutions to previously insurmountable challenges.

This chapter provides the groundwork for applying

generative AI to solve complex scientific problems.

www.ingramcontent.com/pod-product-compliance
Lightning Source LLC
LaVergne TN
LVHW051701050326
832903LV00032B/3942